C000003180

Swansea

REMEMBERED

South Wales Evening Post

Swansea
REMEMBERED

DAVID ROBERTS

The Breedon Books
Publishing Company
Derby

First published in Great Britain by
The Breedon Books Publishing Company Limited
Breedon House, 3 The Parker Centre, Derby, DE21 4SZ. 2000

© SOUTH WALES EVENING POST, 2000

All Rights Reserved. No part of this publication may be reproduced, stored in a retrieval
system, or transmitted in any form, or by any means, electronic, mechanical,
photocopying, recording or otherwise without the prior permission in writing of the
copyright holders, nor be otherwise circulated in any form or binding or cover other
than in which it is published and without a similar condition being imposed on the
subsequent publisher.

ISBN 1 85983 204 0

Printed and bound by Butler & Tanner Ltd., Selwood Printing Works, Caxton Road,
Frome, Somerset.

Colour separations and jacket printing by
GreenShires Group Ltd., Leicester.

Contents

An Appreciation

Many of the photographs in this book have been drawn from the pictorial archives of the *South Wales Evening Post*, but many others are included due to the willingness of residents of Swansea, past and present, to share once again their nostalgic photographs of days gone by.

Some have contributed just one photograph, others lots more; their co-operation is equally valuable.

Additionally, the author and the *South Wales Evening Post* thank the following;

David Beynon
Ivor Davies
Len Pitson
Betty Forshaw
Lemuel Shapton
Pat Hughes
Hywel Morris
John Peake
Brian Jeffries
Jenn Milne
Bob Rigdon
Tony Gigg
Huw Clements
Roy Kneath
Cheryl Roberts
Bernard Morris

Foreword

CHANGE comes in many forms, sometimes sudden, sometimes gradual. It always brings new memories.

But these fade – so it is useful to have a reminder.

Following on from its companion volumes, *Images of Swansea* and *Memory Lane Swansea,* this book provides an intriguing look at the people, places and events of the past.

Its wonderful pictures will revive many forgotten moments.

Now that Swansea has stepped boldly into the 21st Century, the collection is a proud reflection of the way our city used to be.

The *South Wales Evening Post* is delighted to present *Swansea Remembered* and is grateful to the readers and contributors who made the book possible.

George Edwards,
Editor
South Wales Evening Post

Swansea – the Start

SWANSEA'S development from sleepy settlement to vibrant city has been open to many influences.

It's location has always been convenient for shipping … and for invasion. As a result its early history was not peaceful and, ever since, it's people have never lacked energy.

The origin of the word Swansea is open to debate but it was first officially used in 1738, a time when copper smelting was laying the foundations of the area's industrial heritage.

Other industries also flourished as the town grew into an important industrialised port.

Now, with the demise of heavy industry and maritime power, there are more major changes on the horizon.

The people of Swansea have emerged from more than 900 years of change to see their city fixed firmly on the world map.

And today's citizens seem determined to make their own mark on their community's long history.

Along the Way

Swansea's first sweet shop – Powe's at the corner of Orange Street, 1870.

Mansel Street around 1855 with Heathfield House on the left in the background and the Deaf and Dumb Institution on the right.

An 1880 view of the site across the road from Swansea Museum.

Gower Street, in the early 1900s.

The Theatre Royal, Temple Street, 1898.

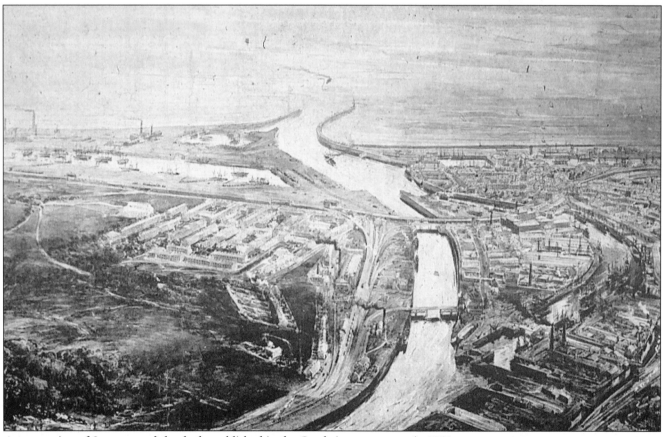

An engraving of Swansea and the docks published in the Cambrian newspaper in 1881.

Swansea's first General Post Office, Castle Bailey Street, in the early 1900s.

High Street, 1900.

Swansea Fruit
Market, Alexandra
Road, 1900.

Oxford Street,
about 1900, looking
out from its
junction with
Union Street.

Swansea Castle, 1904.

Prospect Place, looking towards Wind Street, 1908.

Wind Street, showing the monument which occupied pride of place in 1912.

The tram terminus at High Street, 1912. The site of the Hotel Cameron is now occupied by an Argos store

The entrance to Victoria Park, 1920. This is now the site of Swansea Guildhall.

Brynymor Road, 1920, with an ex-Weston-Super-Mare tram on its way to Brynmill.

Traffic waits for the North dock drawbridge to open in 1922. The bridge was lifted by hydraulic rams then cables drew it back across rollers to allow ships to pass.

St Mary's Church, Swansea, early 1920s. The structure was wrecked by World War Two bombing then re-built.

Union Street, early 1920s.

Looking from the forecourt of High Street station across into Alexandra Road, 1925.

Castle Street, looking south from High Street, 1925.

Castle Street, looking north, 1925. The double deck tram has just arrived from Morriston.

The Ben Evans store, Castle Bailey Street, mid-1920s. It stood on the site of the modern Castle Square.

F. W. Woolworth's 3d & 6d store in 1930 High Street. The Argos store is here now.

Looking from Castle Street towards High Street, 1930.

Early 1930s view of Picton House which stood roughly where the Dillwyn Street roundabout is.

An aerial view of 1934 Swansea showing Castle Street in the centre and the North Dock across the top of the picture.

Excitement in St Helen's Road as Swansea's 'Big Sir' fire engine answers an emergency call in 1937.

This is how the *South Wales Daily Post* of Wednesday, June 30, 1937 pictured the crowd which gathered along the route of Swansea's last trams. It shows two cars that operated a special service between Swansea Hospital and Wind Street on June 29, to raise funds for the hospital.

Looking from Castle Street down towards Wind Street, 1946.

Levelled bomb sites provided useful parking space as this view towards Castle Street on August 6, 1948, shows.

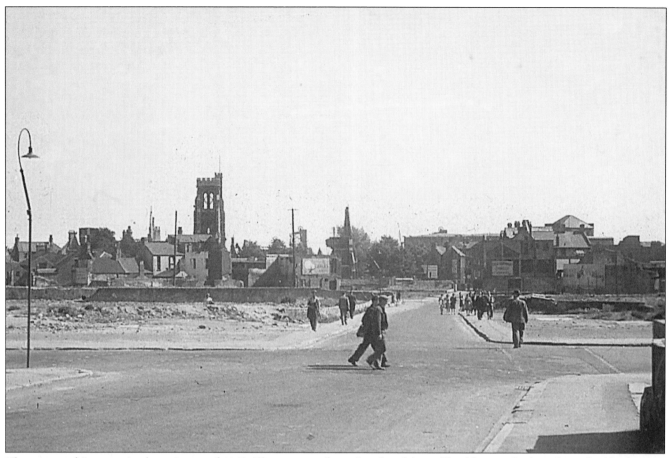

The centre of Swansea in the summer of 1949. The ravages of wartime bombing still evident at the junction of Oxford Street and Waterloo Street. The tower of the blitzed St Mary's Church stands in the background.

Alexandra Road as it greeted rail travellers when they left High Street station in 1950. Wartime bomb damage is still visible.

Nissen huts were erected to serve as shops after World War Two. These were in use in Oxford Street in the early 1950s.

Workmen removing the North Dock bridge structure during the mid-1950s to enable the creation of the modern Quay Parade dual carriageway. The bridge had been out of use since 1928.

The corner of Oxford Street, looking into Union Street, in the early 1950s. This is now the site of jewellers H. Samuel.

Wassail Square, 1958. It was demolished to make way for the Quadrant Centre development. Garden Street to the left is now a multi-storey car park.

Dyfatty Flats with a thriving dockside panorama in the 1958.

Quay Parade, with its railway arches and Weaver's flour mill, 1960. The Weaver's site is now occupied by Sainsbury's supermarket car park.

Quay Parade and the old River Tawe bridge heading eastwards, 1960. St Thomas is in the background.

Looking towards Hafod from the high-level railway bridge that stood alongside the River Tawe road bridge, 1960.

Castle Gardens in early summer, 1960.

Railways once criss-crossed Swansea. This was the scene alongside Victoria Road as steam gave way to diesel power in 1963. The cement lorry hides a bridge which stood at the bottom of Wind Street.

Construction work on the Victoria Road dual carriageway, looking westwards, during the early 1960s. Swansea Museum is on the left while the demolished railway arches march off towards Paxton Street rail depot and the line to Shrewsbury.

The Plaza cinema on The Kingsway, shortly before it closed in 1965.

Demolition men at work on the Plaza cinema in April 1965.

The newly-opened pedestrian subway from Prospect Place to Wind Street, mid-1966. Coleridge House stands near the subway entrance. The site is now a car park.

Looking down Wind Street, 1967.

Wind Street from the high-level railway bridge that spanned its bottom end, April 1967. The Metropole Garage and Rialto Cinema are on the left.

Looking from Adelaide Street towards York Place and Princess Way, 1967.

Railway arches along Quay Parade, 1967. This was the main road eastwards out of the city.

The entrance to The Strand from Quay Parade, 1967.

Oystermouth Road and the Bay View Hotel, 1968. The vehicles on the right are parked on the trackbed of the former Mumbles Railway while the raised area alongside them is the trackbed of the Swansea Victoria to Shrewsbury line.

A bird's-eye view of 1969 Swansea.

A 1970s aerial view of Swansea around St Helen's rugby and cricket ground.

Filling in the North Dock basin, 1970. The area in the foreground, is now Sainsbury's supermarket.

The Strand with its disused railway arches, 1972.

Castle Gardens, 1974. Boots, in the centre, is now McDonalds restaurant.

The former Swansea Victoria railway station site is cleared in preparation for the construction of Swansea Leisure Centre in 1975.

Swansea Guildhall, mid-1970s.

Soar Chapel and Greenhill Post Office in 1976 shortly before the fire-damaged chapel was demolished. This is now the site of the busy Dyfatty road junction.

The partly demolished Metropole Garage, Wind Street, 1975.

An intriguing view of Wind Street from the top of the former Post Office, late 1970s.

The BT tower dwarfs surrounding buildings in The Strand, late 1970s.

Looking towards Swansea docks in 1978. The former Docks Board offices and *Evening Post* buildings in Adelaide Street can be seen in the centre.

Castle Street, 1978.

Swansea Leisure Centre in 1978, with much of the Maritime Quarter still to be developed.

Looking across Swansea city centre towards Mount Pleasant in 1978.

Princess Way in the late 1970s, before it was pedestrianised.

A rare view of Swansea Castle with the roof tops of Wind Street in the foreground, 1978.

Looking down on The Kingsway Circle pedestrian subway system, late 1970s.

Pride of the People

The residents of Bishopston turn out for their 1913 carnival.

Young riflemen at Bishopston, 1915, as World War One raged in Europe.

Swansea Borough policemen outside Fforestfach police station, 1920.

Swansea Borough Police on duty at the Royal Welsh Show, Carmarthen, August 1925.

The ladies choir at the 1926 Royal National Eisteddfod, held at Swansea.

Swansea Borough Police force band, 1931.

A group of cornet players and their bandmaster at Victoria Park, 1932.

Swansea General Hospital staff, late 1930s. The hospital stood between St Helen's Road and Phillips Parade.

Swansea (Wesley) Sea Scouts about to set off for summer camp at Pembroke, 1938.

Sketty Home Guard detachment, 1941, as World War Two continued.

Parc Beck nurses, 1944.

The Home Guard detachment at Baldwins & Elba works, Crymlyn Burrows, in front of the cricket pavilion, 1944.

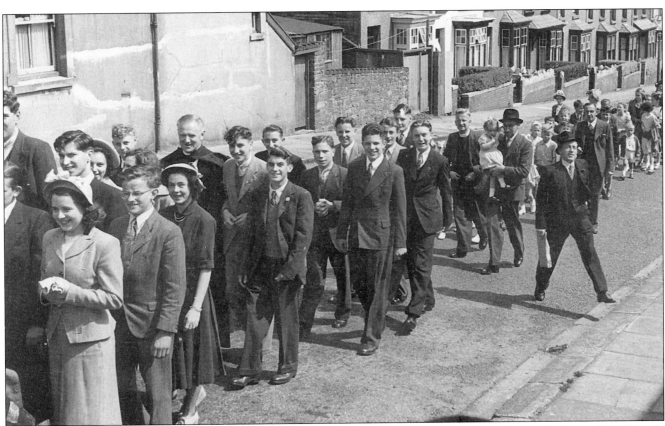

A Whitsun procession in 1948, made up of churches and chapels in Manselton. In the foreground are members of St Michael's and All Angels Church. The procession ended in a service at Manselton Park.

Swansea Sea Cadets, August 1948.

Swansea General Hospital nursing students at St James Church, November 1956.

Tin soldiers in the Sketty Church pantomime Tom, Tom, The Piper's Son which was staged in January 1952.

Swansea School of Art & Crafts students and staff at their June 1958 fashion show.

Another look at 1958 fashions from Swansea School of Arts & Crafts.

Sketty Scouts and Cubs, 1964.

Mayor of Swansea, Councillor T R Davies at a civic march past in 1966 accompanied by civic officers and dignataries.

Sketty Scouts, 1966.

Swansea Air Training Corps, 1969.

The cast of the pantomime *Robinson Crusoe* at the Grand Theatre, Swansea, with stars Stan Stennett, Johnny Tudor and Ronae Coyles, 26 December 1969.

Lord Mayor of Swansea, Lillian Hopkin, presents the Freedom of Swansea to officers and crew of the Mumbles Lifeboat, 1986.

Around the Districts

The Promenade, Southend, Mumbles, 1898.

Mayals Lane, Blackpill, late 1890s.

The entrance to Singleton Park at the bottom of Brynmill Lane, before 1900.

Looking downhill past the thatched cottage towards Brynmill Square, pre-1900.

The Arcade, Waunarlwydd, pre-1900.

A Swansea-bound tram leaves the Commercial pub at the junction of Eaton Road and Llangyfelach Road, Pentre Estyll, about 1910.

Bonymden Windmill, 1900. It was demolished in 1966.

Mynyddbach Chapel about 1910. It was here that the Bard Gwyrosydd wrote the words to the hymn *Calon Lan*

Summer chalets at Plunch Lane, Limeslade, 1912.

Oxwich, 1915.

Woodfield Street, Morriston, 1905.

Townhill, 1925.

Penclawdd, 1937.

The ruined windmill on the cliff above Caswell Bay, mid-1920s.

Ashleigh Road, Blackpill, 1925.

Sketty Cross, 1939.

Parkmill, showing Shepherd's Stores, 1947.

Dick Slade, Mumbles, about 1950.

Broadway, Sketty, 1952.

Heol Ddu, Llansamlet, mid-1950s.

J G Clement's Pharmacy, Cwmbwrla, 1955.

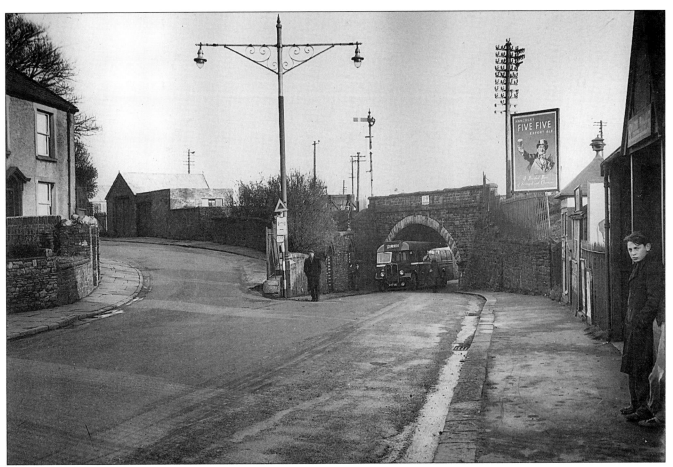

The junction of Ysgol Street and Port Tennant Road, Port Tennant, 1957.

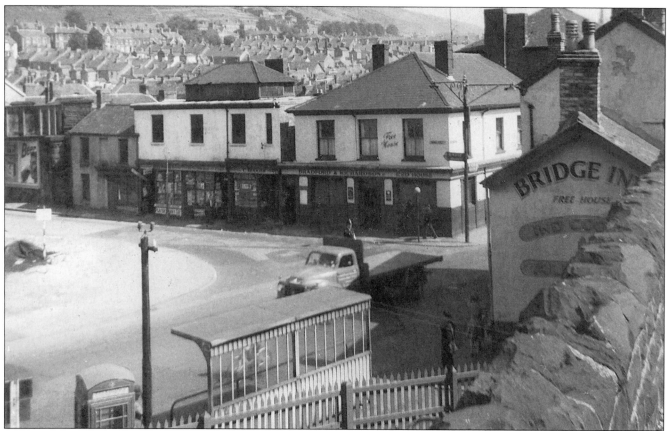

The Red House pub and Bridge Inn, at the junction of Thomas Street and Fabian Street, St Thomas, June 1960.

Fabian Street, St Thomas, 1960.

Wimmerfield Crescent, Killay, under construction during 1960.

Thomas Street, St Thomas, looking towards Pentreguinea Road, 1960.

Clyne Court flats, built by Wimpey at Sketty Park in 1962. Much surrounding housing had yet to be constructed.

The junction of Derwen Fawr Road and Mumbles Road, Blackpill, 1964.

Gowerton, 1967.

Cwmrhydyceirw Quarry, Morriston, 1970.

The River Tawe at low water in 1972. Construction of the river barrage means it is a view seldom seen today as the water level remains high. This view is from the New Cut bridge. Now a second bridge spans the view.

The former Scala Cinema, St Thomas, 1977.

Woodfield Street, Morriston, 1984 showing St John's Church in the middle of the road.

Younger Days

Blackpill School, 1899.

Lonlas Council School, 1913.

Standard 4 Brynhyfryd Boys' School, 1916.

Bishopston
School, 1917.

Standard 7 Lonlas Council School, 1925.

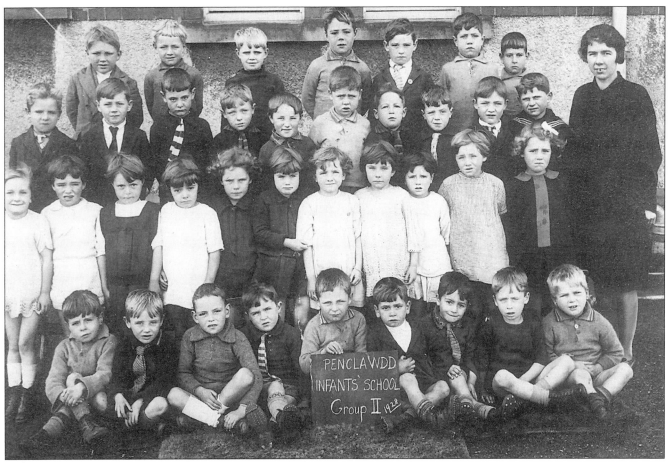

Penclawdd Infants' School, 1928.

Waun Wen Girls' School, 1928.

Standard 5 Oxford Street Boys' School, 1929.

Manselton Infants' School class 1 boys, 1929.

Manselton Infants' School class 2 girls, 1929.

Brynhyfryd Infants' School class 3A, 1933.

Craigcefnparc Primary School, 1933.

Children of Dyfatty Infants School with their toy animals, 1936.

Dyfatty Infants School class 4, 1939.

Standard 4 Cadle School, May 1940.

Powys Avenue School with teacher Mr Charles, 1941.

Pupils of Swansea Grammar School on a trip to France, summer 1950.

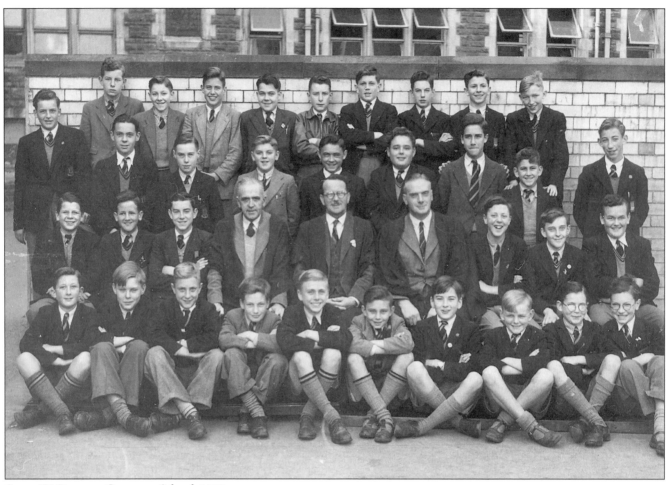

Form 3D Dynevor Grammar School, 1953.

Newton Church School, 1953.

Youngsters and their mums tramp through the snow of February 1954 on their way to Sketty school.

Swansea School of Arts & Crafts, spring term, 1956.

Form 5D Dynevor Grammar School, 1956.

Graig School, 1957.

Pupils at Sketty Primary School, 1960.

Terrace Road School, Mount Pleasant, December 1960. Tycoch Junior School, 1960.

Tycoch Junior School, 1960.

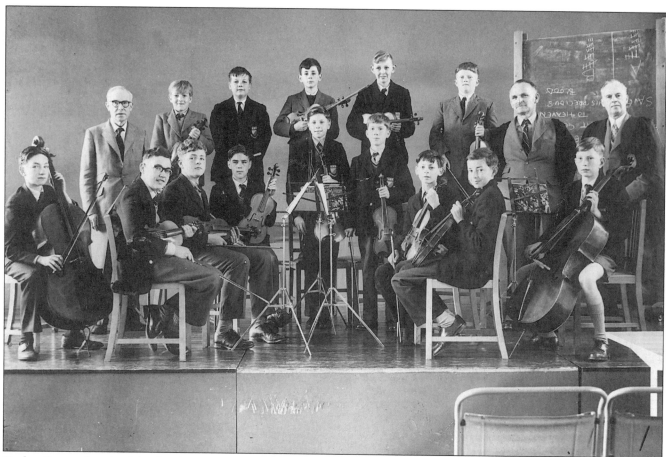

Penlan Comprehensive School string group, 1960.

Danygraig School, early 1960s.

Nelson Street Nursery School, 1961.

Glanmor Girls School pupils with head teacher Miss Hunt, 1961.

First year boys at Bishop Gore School, 1961.

Mynyddbach School pupils set sail from Swansea docks aboard the *SS Devonia* bound for a Mediterranean cruise, 1962.

Swansea University chemistry department, 1963.

Tycoch Junior School, Sketty, 1964.

Coco the Clown has a captive audience at Killay Primary school with his road safety advice in November 1965.

Mynyddbach Girls School seen preparing for an educational cruise aboard the *SS Nevasa* in 1966.

The class of 1967 at Gowerton Girls Grammar School.

Dunvant Infants School class 4, May 1968.

Dunvant Infants School, 1970.

Morriston Comprehensive School, 1972.

Headteacher Owen Lewis with staff at Gowerton Girls Grammar School, 1973.

Participants in a West Glamorgan Education Authority brass band course at Dan-y-Coed music centre, West Cross, November 1977.

Form 4 Dynevor Comprehensive School, 1978.

Working Ways

Miners at Pwll-Y-Cordyn pit, Llansamlet, early 1900s, along with one fascinated young girl.

Swansea postmen, 1904.

Miners at Clyne Valley, 1913.

Women cockle gatherers head for home after an arduous shift on the Loughor Estuary at Penclawdd, 1920s.

These were some of the men who erected the telegraph poles and the telephone lines in 1923 Swansea and surrounding districts.

Mumbles lighthouse keeper Johnny Thomas with the compressed air machinery that powered its fog horn in the 1920s.

A team of divers at Swansea docks, 1925.

The blacksmith's shop in Plymouth Street, late 1920s.

Richard Thomas & Baldwin's tinplate workers at the King's Dock works, 1929.

Swansea General Hospital laundry, late 1920s.

Some of the construction workers employed by contractors C Sansom who helped build Townhill's homes in the early 1930s.

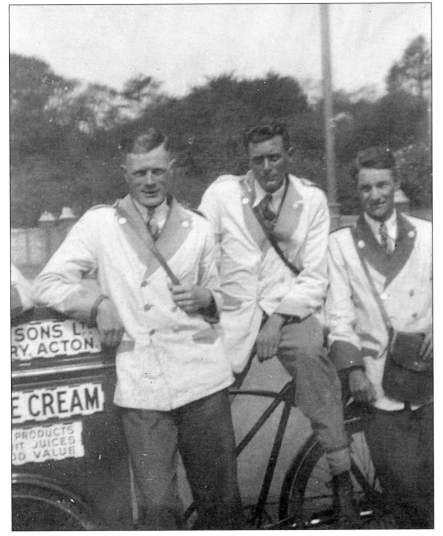

These ice cream salesmen peddled their wares and their bikes during the long hot summers of the 1930s.

Timber scaffolding erected by Bennett Bros workmen in Terrace Road, Mount Pleasant in the early 1930s.

Railwaymen take a break at the LMS Paxton Street locomotive depot in 1939.

Swansea East Dock locomotive depot Mutual Improvement Class including men from Danygraig depot, 1940.

Some of the dedicated women who ran a troop canteen at Alexandra Road during World War Two.

A group of fitters, machinists and apprentices at the fitting shop of the Upper Forest & Worcester tinplate works, 1942.

Swansea fish market, 1950.

Tailors at work sat on the square yard of table they rented at Hodge's menswear factory, Fforestfach, 1950.

Taking a break at Hughes & Morgan, 1950.

Workshop staff at Hughes & Morgan South dock box and container makers, 1950.

Locomen at Danygraig, 1950s.

Swansea dry dock workers, June 1951.

Early construction work at Velindre Tinplate works, 1951.

Some of the women staff of confectionery manufacturers Fred Holt & Sons, Orange Street, 1951.

The Woolworth's High Street cafeteria crew who fed countless hungry shoppers in the mid-1950s.

Employees of Swansea Garages, Fforestfach, 1956.

Katie, the friendly proprietor of The Cosy Café
at Swansea's post-war market, 1957.

Nurses at Cefn Coed Hospital, 1958.

Production staff of the Pressed Steel Company at Jersey Marine, on Friday, 4 March 1960, the first anniversary of the laying of the cornerstone. The works later became the Ford plant and then Visteon.

Model vehicles galore with some of the women who made them at Mettoy, Fforestfach, in the early 1960s.

Danygraig locomotive depot staff during the 1960.

Mettoy despatch and warehouse workers in the 1960s.

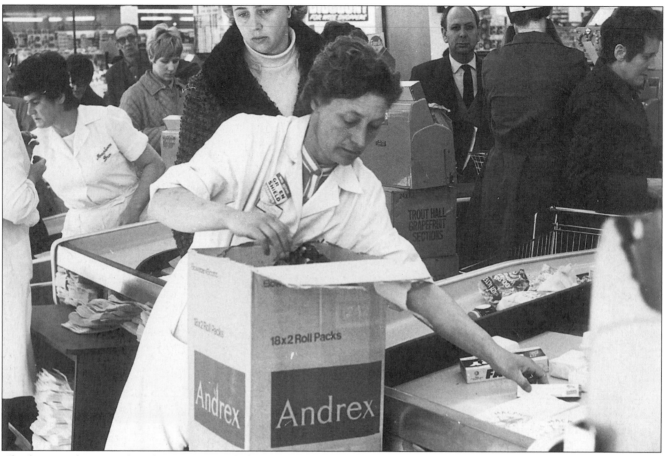

Checkout workers were kept busy at Swansea's first supermarket, Macpherson's in Oxford Street in 1964.

In-store bakeries are nothing new: Macphersons led the way in 1964.

Signalman Bryan Lewis at the busy Burrows signal box, 1963.

Labour Party canvassers including Aberavon MP John Morris, threw their weight behind the successful 1964 campaign of Alan Williams for the Swansea West parliamentary seat. Here they are seen canvassing in Dyfed Avenue, Townhill.

The backstage crew who operated the fly ropes at the Grand Theatre, 1966.

The 'Bottom End' maintenance team at Swansea docks, 1968.

There was no shortage of baked beans at Macpherson's supermarket in 1969 as they stacked 'em high and sold 'em cheap. This lorry alone contained 80,000 tins and there was another behind! Plenty of reason for a special photograph.

Staff at George J. Marin's
Lower Oxford Street garage,
1972.

The Grand Theatre
stage crew, 1972.

Beside the Seaside

Swansea Beach and West Pier. 1896.

Crowds throng Mumbles Head in the late 1890s.

Caswell Bay, 1902.

Horse-drawn bathing huts on Swansea beach, early 1900s.

Langland Bay, 1905.

Swansea Beach, 1908.

Crowds gather at The Slip railway crossing ready to spill on to Swansea sands, 1910.

Mumbles Pier, 1912.

Three Cliffs Bay, 1913.

Picnic time on Caswell Beach, 1913.

Swansea Promenade, opposite the Recreation Ground, early 1920s.

A family picnic, Pwll Du Bay, Gower, 1923.

On the sands at Loughor, 1925.

Motorists rendezvous at Limeslade during the 1930s.

Sunny summer days were a delight for ice cream seller Bert Williams in 1930 … and those who stopped him to buy one!

Family holidays in a chalet at Caswell meant the obligatory 'one for the album' even in 1949.

Deck chair days on the sand near the slip, 1949.

Selling cockles on the sands near the Slip bridge, late 1940s.

Langland Bay, early 1950s.

Time for playing with dad on Swansea sands near the Slip, 1961.

Rotherslade meant a chance to ride on the donkeys in the 1960s.

Boating at Southend, Mumbles, 1960s.

Oystermouth, near Knals Rock, 1965.

Away from it All

A party of Mumbles Railway employees off for a day out in 1910.

A group of Mumbles men all dressed up and ready to go for a day's outing, about 1919.

The licensee of the Cuba Hotel off for a spin with his family in the early 1920s.

The charabanc was the way to go for these Swansea friends in the 1920s.

Camping in Gower 1920s-style.

Manselton neighbours all set for a paddle steamer trip to Ilfracombe, 1923.

Packed in on a 1930s paddle steamer from Swansea to Ilfracombe.

Swansea families on a day out at Ilfracombe, 1930s.

A caravan holiday in Oxwich, 1932.

Family fun, 1930s style at Bracelet Bay, Mumbles. The wooden horse was a popular photographic prop.

Albert Hall cinema employees on a day trip to Porthcawl, September 1946.

Heol-y-Gors Young People's holiday convention at Tiverton, Devon, August 1946.

Residents of Townhill Gardens off to the seaside, 1946.

Louis Marx toy factory press shop girls on a 1948 outing to Weston-Super-Mare, 1948.

This group of workers from the Baldwin's & Elba works went to support the Swans at Brighton in 1948.

Workers from Richard Thomas & Baldwin's on a trip to London, May 1949.

Rhoose youth camp was the destination for this group from Swansea YMCA in 1949.

These Hodges Menswear factory workers travelled to Cardiff to support the Swans in September 1949.

This YMCA group posed for the cameraman at High Street station before leaving for an early 1950s excursion.

A Sunday outing to Porthcawl for staff of the Albert Hall cinema, 1952.

Members of Elim Church, Orchard Street, have a lift aboard a farm trailer at Llangennith, 1951.

Cabinet makers from the Strand head off for the day in the early 1950s.

Weston-Super-Mare beckoned for Danygraig locomens' improvers class, 1950.

These Swansea friends had the time of their lives at Butlin's Pwllheli, in the summer of 1952.

Addis workers all set for a 1950s summer coach outing.

Members of St Thomas Ratepayers' Association and their families ready to board their coaches for a mid-1950s away day.

Swansea Schoolboys AFC with trainer Dai Beynon before boarding the train that took them to London and West Ham in the mid-1950s.

Regulars from the Swansea Castle pub off to Tintern Abbey, Gloucestershire, 1955.

Rees & Kirby employees enjoyed a day at Hay-on-Wye in 1956.

Campbell's Oxford Street furniture store staff at Ross-on-Wye, 1958.

Victoria Park OAP group on a 1960s excursion.

The Villiers Arms womens' darts team all dressed up and ready to leave for a 1980s day out.

Harbour boatman William Shreeve gave his children a day out on a launch in Swansea docks in 1970.

Special Occasions

A wedding group outside the Valley Hotel, Bishopston, 1917.

Getting married-1920-style in Bishopston.

This World War One tank certainly drew the crowds when it was trundled down High Street in 1920.

The crowd waits patiently at Singleton Park for the start of the 1925 Proclamation Ceremony for the 1926 Swansea and District Royal National Eisteddfod.

The Gorsedd Bards assemble at the Proclamation Ceremony in Singleton Park in 1925 for the following year's Swansea and District National Eisteddfod.

A mid-1920s wedding at Birchgrove.

George and Annie John with some of their family after their 1930 wedding at Danygraig Chapel.

Guests spill down the steps of Mount Calvary Chapel, Port Tennant, in 1932.

The top end of Rodney Street celebrated the 1937 Coronation of George VI with a street tea party.

A Townhill wedding, 1940.

Swansea wedding fashion, 1946-style.

VE Day celebration in the backyard of the Brooklands Hotel, Oxford Street, 1945.

A farewell presentation at Louis Marx toy factory, Fforestfach, 1948.

Gendros School pupils dressed up to celebrate the Festival of Britain, 1951.

A Swansea carnival procession to mark the Coronation of Queen Elizabeth II, 1953.

Fancy dress Coronation celebrations for these lads at Siloh Crescent, Brynhyfryd, 1953. Is that the Queen on her 'throne' behind the boys?

Crowds line The Kingsway for the visit of the Queen in the mid-1950s.

The staff of Woolworth's High Street joined the crowds as the Queen toured Swansea during her mid-1950s visit.

St Thomas Community Centre staged this pantomime in the mid-1950s.

Coronation celebrations at Cwm Road, Hafod, 1953.

Pant Street, Port Tennant, on parade for the Coronation, 1953.

Bathurst Street children with a fancy dress contribution to their 1953 Coronation street party.

The retirement of Charles Wills at Hodges' Menswear factory, Fforestfach, 1959.

Residents of Clyne Court, Sketty Park, turn out to celebrate the investiture of the Prince of Wales, 1969.

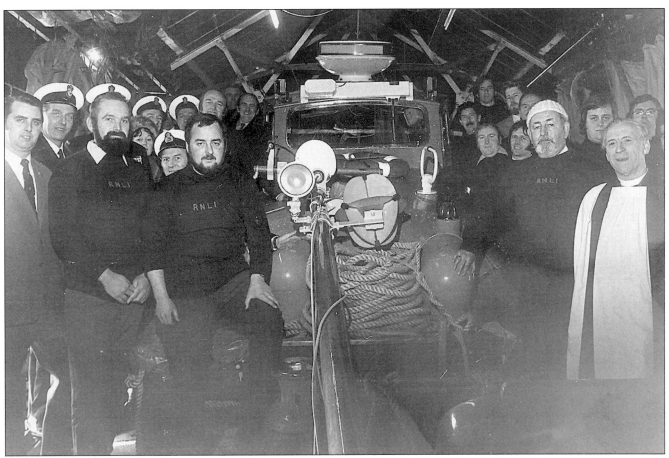

The rededication ceremony of the Mumbles lifeboat William Gammon, in the lifeboat house after it had been refurbished and fitted with radar in 1972.

The official opening of Penrice Guide hut, 1975.

Upper Killay carnival, 1975.

Gower Cub Scouts plant a tree on Swansea promenade for Operation Greenleaf, 1979 with a little help from the Mayor Councillor Susan Jones.

Residents of Derlwyn, Dunvant, celebrate the Jubilee of Queen Elizabeth II, 1977.

Jasmine Close, Sketty Park celebrates the wedding of Prince Charles and Lady Diana Spencer, 1981.

Our Lady of Lourdes Church members with their carnival float at Townhill, 1990.

Moving Along

The naming ceremony of the Swansea lifeboat, *Wolverhampton*, 1866.

Looking across the South Dock in the late 1890s. The view is from a point where the Marriott Hotel stands today towards Townhill.

Passengers board the Rhossili to Swansea bus, 1910.

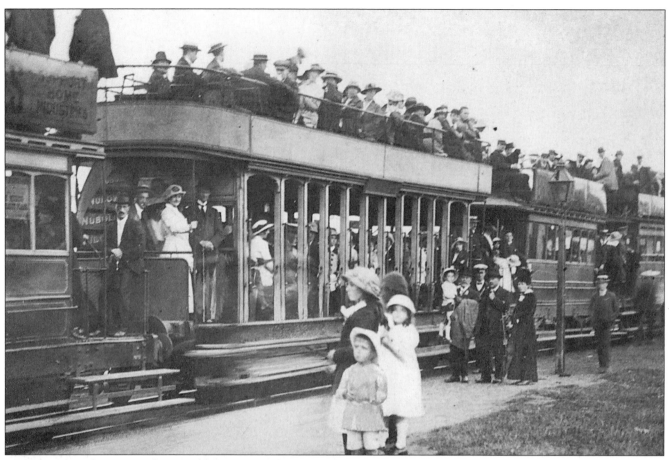

Sunny summer days meant the Mumbles train was always packed in 1910.

The Mumbles Train, 1912.

The Great Western Railway South Dock goods depot, also known as Burrows Lodge yard, 1912.

This Bishopston Motor Service bus was all decked out for carnival day around 1912.

The Swan Motor Service ferried passengers to and from Gower in 1920.

Roadworkers at Bishopston, early 1920s.

Webb's bakery van, Gorseinon, in the early 1920s.

The Mumbles Train leaves Rutland Street for the pier, mid-1920s.

A steam lorry on Mumbles Road, Blackpill, 1927.

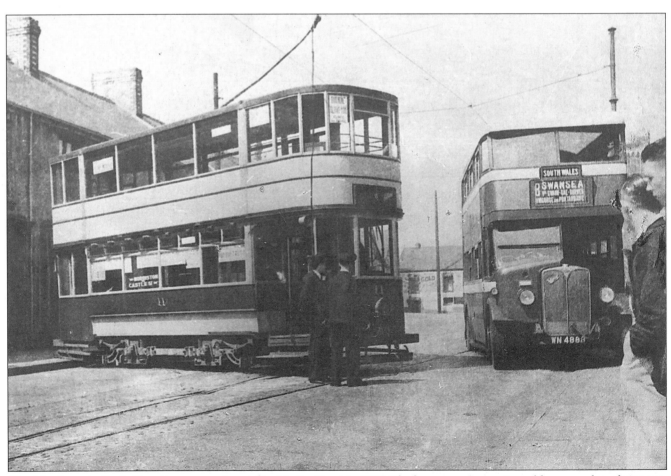

The Morriston to Castle Street tram came to grief in Martin Street in 1930. The bus squeezing past would soon replace the trams.

The Swansea tram depot at St Helen's Road, early 1930s.

The Gardiner coal lorry that was a familiar sight in 1938 Danygraig.

This young Greenhill lad had a while to go before he could reach the pedals of this 1936 delivery bicycle.

Killay Station, near today's Railway Inn, 1938.

Swansea docks, late 1940s.

Oil tankers at Queen's Dock, Swansea, 1947.

A line up of AEC Regal III coaches at South Wales Transport's Ravenhill depot, 1949.

If any South Wales Transport buses or coaches broke down, John Cooke, his workmates at the Ravenhill depot and their heavy duty breakdown truck would be sent to help in 1949.

The workshop of Bassett's garage at Greenfield Street, Swansea, with a selection of the vehicles they sold, mid-1950s.

These gleaming models in the mid-1950s car showroom of Arthur Bassett, at Greenfield Street, were all classics of the future.

One of RP Culley's beer delivery wagons that were a familiar sight around Swansea and beyond in the mid-1950s.

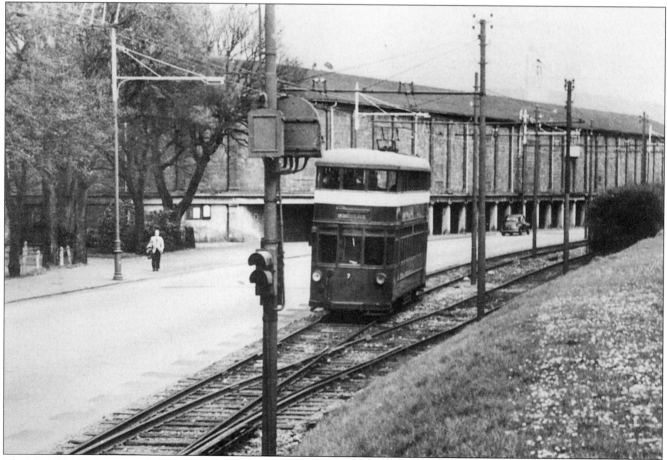

The Mumbles Train passes St Helen's rugby and cricket ground, mid-1950s.

A train from Shrewsbury heads into Swansea Victoria station during the late 1950s with St Helen's rugby ground in the background.

A local train heading along Swansea seashore from Victoria Station to Pontarddulais, mid-1950s. The track of the Mumbles Railway can be seen on the left.

A South Wales Transport AEC double decker on its route to and from Sketty and Uplands in 1959.

The last journey of the Mumbles Train, January 5, 1960.

Riding on this rag and bone man's horse was the ultimate in cowboys and Indians for this youngster in 1959 Page Street.

This Paddington to Swansea express made an impressive sight for the photographer as it crossed Landore viaduct on the approach to Swansea High Street station in the early 1960s.

An atmospheric early 1960s night-time peep into Landore's busy main line locomotive depot.

The Mumbles lifeboat William Gammon leaves the slipway after a 1970s launch.

A slipway view of the Mumbles lifeboat Pentland, 1974.

United We Stand

Sir John T Dillwyn-Llewellyn and Cwmbwrla's St John's Ward committee for the 1895 parliamentary election.

The massed choir at the 1926 Royal National Eisteddfod at Singleton Park.

Brynhyfryd Baptist Chapel choir, early 1930s.

Swansea St Mary's Guide company, 1933.

Alf Thomas's Hafod concert party, 1936.

These friends were photographed at the last Swansea hospital carnival, 1939.

Wartime evacuees from Swansea pictured in the comparative safety of West Wales.

The Lewis Lewis store ladies' choir with accompanist Howard Lewis and Gwyneth Lewis, granddaughter of the shop's founder, 1947.

Swansea Ranger Guides in Penrice, Gower, 1949.

The annual Scouts dance at the Brangwyn Hall, 1949.

Young guests at a children's ball at the Brangwyn Hall, early 1950s.

A group of Addis workers enjoy a 1950s night out.

Some of the members of the Sketty Club, Eversley Road, 1952.

Danygraig locomotive depot men enjoy a few pints in the early 1950s.

A civic visit for members of Brynhyfryd Baptist Chapel, early 1950s.

Swansea Dramatic Society members at their annual dinner, 1951.

The Caswell Bay Hotel was the venue in 1952 for the first staff dinner of the Pascoe group of companies.

The Young Peoples' Guild of St Paul's Church, Sketty, in the vicarage grounds, 1952.

Cast of the 1952 pantomime at Soar Chapel, Dyfatty.

Conductor Brynog Jones with the Tawe Choral Society, 1954.

Managers, departmental heads and staff welfare committee members at Swansea Co-operative Retail Society's dinner, 1955.

Albert Hall cinema staff get together with comedian Stan Stennett, 1955.

Residents of Upper King's Head Road, Gendros, in 1955 fancy dress mood.

Members of Morriston Orpheus Choir carry off the cup at the 1955 Pwllheli National Eisteddfod.

The Merry Boys concert party at Townhill Community Centre, mid-1950s.

A Post Office Christmas party, 1956, again with comedian Stan Stennet.

Party time at the Flying Angel Seamen's Mission, Christmas 1957.

St Thomas Ratepayers' Association at the community centre, 1958.

Swansea and West Wales branch members of the Association of Ophthalmic Practitioners held their annual dinner at the Dragon Hotel, 1962.

Post Office workers at a 1960s tramps ball.

The 1967 Christmas party of the Lewis Lewis store at the Dolphin Hotel, Whitewalls.

Dunvant Townswomen's Guild members in a music and dance routine at the Patti Pavilion, 1969.

Mumbles lifeboat crewmen and officials on the boathouse slipway, early 1970s.

A group of Mettoy factory workers at their 1972 Christmas party.

The mid-1980s saw this group of Swansea Oxfam workers spreading the good word to Cherbourg, France.

Easter 1988 and the
bonnets sold like wildfire
at the Oxfam shop at
Morriston.

The 100th anniversary
get-together of former pupils of
Swansea High School, late 1980s.

That Sporting Spirit

Morriston Thursday Cricket Club, 1911.

The Welsh Juniors AFC, 1919-20.

Swansea RFC seconds, 1919-20.

Regatta day at Mumbles, early 1920s.

Swansea Town AFC, 1920-21.

Swansea Town AFC, 1921-22.

Swansea University women's hockey team, 1922-23.

Parc Llewelyn RFC, cup winners, 1925.

Oldwalls Quoits team, 1926.

Otter hunting at Penllergaer, August 1928.

Young boxers at the Gwent Hall, Gwent Road, Townhill, 1930.

St Stephen's Church Football Club, early 1930s.

Cwmbwrla School, Swansea schools' Junior Cricket League champions, 1934.

Swansea's first try scored by Dennis Hunt against New Zealand, September 28, 1935. Final score: Swansea 11pts, New Zealand 3.

Swansea Schools' soccer league team Waun Wen seniors, Hospital Cup finalists at Vetch Field, Jubilee Day, 1935.

Swansea Schools AFC, 1938-39 with Dai Beynon, the trainer who led them to success.

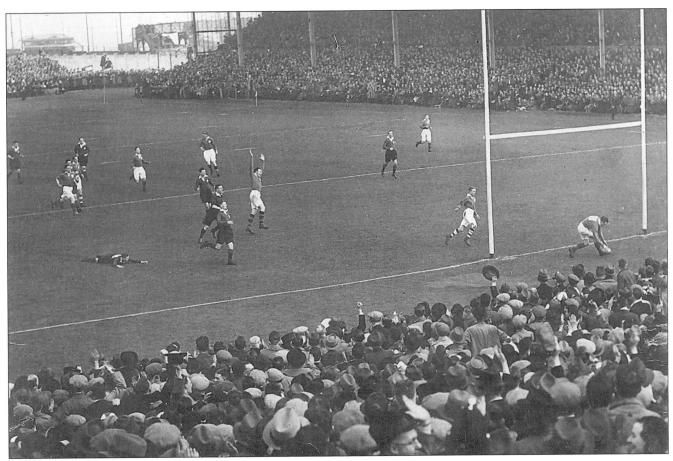

Wales v Ireland at St Helen's ground, 1938.

Cwmbwrla Junior School soccer XI, 1945-46.

Swansea Schools AFC, Welsh Shield winners, 1945-46.

Swansea Schools' AFC Welsh Shield winners, 1948.

Swansea Grammar School Hockey team, 1949.

The back of Nelson Street was the unlikely starting point for an attempt on the Monte Carlo Rally in 1950 by a group of Swansea motoring enthusiasts. They included garage proprietor Arthur Bassett.

Gorseinon Miners Bowls team on tour in the early 1950s.

Hodges Menswear factory rounders team, 1950.

Swansea Schools AFC 1951-52 Welsh Shield winners and English Trophy finalists.

Swansea Grammar School Harriers, with opponents St Athan behind, 1951.

West End FC, 1951-52.

Gorseinon Ladies Bowls team, mid-1950s.

Manselton Hotel Darts team, 1954 after lifting the league title at the Pier Hotel, Mumbles.

Penlan Multilateral School senior soccer B team, 1956-57. The school later became Penlan Comprehensive.

Townhill Community Centre Harlequins, 1957.

Unit Colts, 1958-59 were employees at the Unit Superheater & Pipe company in the Strand.

Mynyddbach School Junior Relay team which represented Swansea Harriers in an early 1960s athletics meeting.

Mettoy Cricket XI, early 1960s.

The rugby XV of Martin Street Boys' School, Morriston, 1965-66.

Dunvant School rugby XV, 1965-66.

AWCO wire works football club, mid-1960s.

Preparing for the annual Boxing Day rowing challenge between the crew of Mumbles' Lifeboat and Mumbles Rowing Club during the 1960s.

Bishop Gore School swimming team, 1965.

Cwmdonkin Bowls Club, Swansea League champions, 1968-69.

The Pier Hotel Pirates darts team, Mumbles Pier, 1969.

Cwmdonkin Bowls Club members, 1970s.

Cwmdonkin Bowls team, summer 1974.

Cefn Hengoed School netball team, 1975.

Tycoch United who beat Mumbles Boys' Club in the 1978 under 16s Corinthian Cup at Vetch Field.

Swansea RFC under 13s 1978-79.

Deputy Lord Mayor Trevor Burtonshaw starts a 1984 charity cycle race.